じゃれマガ

100 Stories of 2018

from the email magazine
by Douglas S. Jarrell
ダグラス・ジャレル

浜島書店

INTRODUCTION

I am happy to publish the 13th book in the Jaremaga series. This year, you'll find stories about the Winter Olympics, an incredible true story about a tour guide who was left behind on a tour, many stories from Hokkaido, and much more. Most of the stories were written by me, but there are some active readers who share their stories with me. I edit their stories and put them up on the Friday Readers' Corner when I can, but there are many stories that don't get sent out. Even if your stories didn't make it to the email magazine, you didn't waste your time. I enjoy reading every story that a reader sends me.

This book is only possible thanks to the support I get from my wife and the people at Hamajima Shoten. I also want to thank my former tap dance club member, Ozaki Kanako, who draws the illustrations for this book. It's wonderful to see the stories through her eyes!

I hope you enjoy reading the stories. I want to encourage people to read in English and learn new English words and expressions. If you want to use this book to improve your English, I suggest you listen to the audio recordings and practice reading them aloud. You can copy the stories in a notebook and make note of new phrases. If you have the time and energy, try writing a similar story and send it to me.

Douglas Jarrell

ジャレル先生の朗読音声を聞こう！
　本書の内容をジャレル先生自身の朗読で聞くことができます。次のホームページにアクセスして，ご利用ください。
http://catchawave.jp/jm/sound2018.html
（2019 年 7 月公開予定）

INDEX

The Power of Education

I'm a third-year student in junior high school. I read about Malala Yousafzai in my English class. She thinks education is very important for children, so she spoke about education at the U.N. on July 12, 2013. She said, "The pen is mightier than the sword." She believes in the power of education. I think education is the only solution for the problems of the world. I want to be a teacher because I want to teach children important things such as, "The pen is mightier than the sword." I believe in Malala and support what she does.

(Written by a reader, Ichikawa Rei)

education 教育　　the U.N. 国際連合(国連)
mightier mighty(強い)の比較級　　solution 解決策

 世界の問題は教育の力で解決できると信じたいです。マララ・ユスフザイさんはその象徴です。この中学生の読者には立派な先生になってほしいと思います。

Tokyo Banana

When my daughter came over for dinner last week, she brought us a present from Tokyo. It was a box of sponge cakes shaped like bananas. Each cake is soft and filled with banana-flavored cream. It reminded me of Twinkies, a popular snack for children in the U.S., but Tokyo Banana is tastier. I wondered how the banana became the symbol of Tokyo. Bananas don't grow this far north. Apparently, the company was looking for a taste that people of all ages liked, and everyone likes the taste of bananas. It has become Tokyo's most popular souvenir.

be filled with 〜　〜でいっぱいである
remind A of 〜　Aに〜のことを連想させる
tastier　tasty（おいしい）の比較級　　apparently　どうも〜らしい
souvenir　みやげ

東京ばな奈は，僕が中学時代に大好きだった
Twinkies というお菓子に似ています。でも僕が
「Twinkies みたい」と言ったら，娘が反発しました。
「Twinkies とは全然違うわ！ 東京ばな奈のほうが
ずっとおいしい！」

Cooking Lobsters

Switzerland has decided to stop restaurants from boiling lobsters alive. Lobsters and other shellfish like crabs and shrimp are often cooked while they are alive. They die in the boiling water, but according to some scientists, this is very slow and painful. With other animals, people are more careful. They try to kill the animals quickly so that they don't feel pain. The Swiss government believes that we should do the same with shellfish. But if cooks don't use boiling water, how can they kill the shellfish? They can put a knife in the lobster's head or use an electric shock.

boil ~ alive ~を生きたままゆでる shellfish 甲殻類
government 政府 electric shock 電気ショック

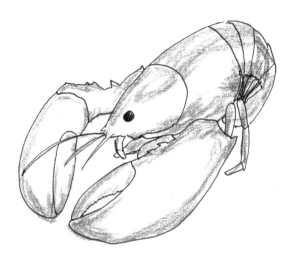

生きているロブスターを沸騰水に入れると痛みを感じているように見えます。生きものを苦しませないように工夫するスイスの考えは分かりますが，調理方法が複雑になりかねません。

Jan. 22, 2018

Japanese First Names Are Difficult!

I went to a conference on Saturday, and I had to introduce five speakers. I didn't have any problems with the Japanese family names. There is only one way to read them. Japanese first names, however, are much more difficult. Although several speakers had common first names, one had a first name that I had never seen before. I went online and checked the name before I left home. I did find the name, but there were SIX different readings! I asked my wife, who is Japanese, but she couldn't help me. In the end, I had to go and ask the speaker how to read his name.

conference　会議　　common　一般的な
go online　インターネットに接続する

Masayuki ?

Masakou ?

Shouyuki? 正 幸

Seikou ?

Shoukou?

日本人の苗字は読めても，名前は本当に分かりません。音読み，訓読み，当て字など選択肢があまりにも多いので，日本人でも自信を持って読める人は少ないと思います。

A Table Tennis Family

A 14-year-old is in the news. Harimoto Tomokazu has become the youngest player to win the Men's Singles at the All-Japan Table Tennis Championships. He beat 28-year-old Mizutani Jun, a 9-time champion and the winner of the bronze medal at the last Olympics. He also won the ITTF World Tour Men's Singles title in the Czech Republic last August. That made him the youngest winner of a World Tour. Actually, Harimoto comes from a table tennis family. His father is a table tennis coach, and his mother played for China in the 1995 World Table Tennis Championships.

the Czech Republic　チェコ共和国

 張本智和選手のように両親が卓球選手だったら，家族と一緒にトレーニングができますね。親の影響は大きいかもしれませんが，張本選手には素質があります。また，彼特有の雄たけびは印象的ですね。

The Coldest Village in the World

   Do you think the winter in Japan is bad? That probably depends on which part of Japan you live in. It is snowy and windy along the Sea of Japan, and the temperatures are very low in Hokkaido, but here in Nagoya, it seldom snows and the temperature usually doesn't go below zero degrees centigrade. In Siberia, it is much colder. People who live in a small village called Oymyakon say that it is the coldest village in the world. The average temperature in January is minus 50 degrees centigrade. It is so cold that the ink in pens freezes, and batteries lose their power. If you go outside, your eyelashes will freeze.

~ degree centigrade　セ氏〜度　　Oymyakon　オイミャコン（村）
eyelash　まつげ

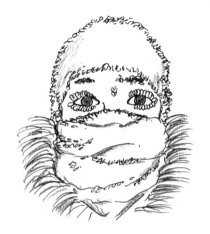

-50℃

世界一寒い村はロシアのシベリアにあります。このような過酷な寒さを一度体験してみたいとは思いますが，僕は寒がりなので実際に耐えられるか心配です。

Freeze the Laundry

Do you know that people in Oymyakon, Siberia (the coldest village in the world), dry laundry in a unique way? They do it by freezing the laundry outside and then removing the ice from the clothes. In this way, the laundry dries in a moment. I live in Hirosaki, which is in the western part of Aomori. It is also cold, and the temperature sometimes goes down to minus 10 degrees. When I was walking to the university this morning, I realized that my runny nose froze. I thought that it might be worthwhile to try drying the laundry by freezing it in Hirosaki, too!

(Written by a reader, Shikama Yuki)

laundry　洗濯物　　remove　取り除く　　runny nose　鼻水
worthwhile　価値がある

Freezing!!

寒い国では乾燥機がなければ洗濯物を乾かすことが
難しいと思っていましたが，もしかするとオイミャ
コン村では名古屋よりも簡単かもしれません。氷さ
え払い落とせば乾きますから。

Total Eclipse of the Moon

Get ready to watch a great performance in the sky. There will be a total lunar eclipse tonight, and the moon will get dark for several hours. How does this happen? The earth moves between the sun and the moon, and the earth's shadow falls on the moon. The moon loses its bright yellow color and becomes a dark red. Tonight the moon will start to change color around 8:50 p.m., and at 10:30 it will be at its darkest. It will get lighter again, and just after midnight the eclipse will be over. If the weather is good in your area, you will be able to see it in the southeast sky.

total eclipse of the moon　皆既月食　　performance　演技，ショー
lunar eclipse　月食

昔は日食や月食と聞くと，空が真っ暗になるのだと思っていました。皆既日食の場合は真っ暗になりますが，皆既月食の場合は月がくすんだ赤色になり，神秘的な夜になります。

Skier from a Small Island

Do you know where Tonga is? It is a small island country in the South Pacific. The country is known for its warm weather and its rugby players, but this year Tonga is sending someone to the PyeongChang Winter Olympics. Pita Taufatofua went to the Rio Summer Olympics two years ago and competed in taekwondo. Then he decided that he wanted to try cross country skiing. He trained on roller skis first and then went to Europe to practice on snow. He qualified in just one year. That is impressive!

qualify　出場資格を得る

ピタ・タウファトファ選手はテコンドーで初めてオリンピックに出場しましたが，次の夏の大会まで待つことができず，ノルディックスキーに挑戦しました。トンガ代表として，夏でも冬でも上半身裸で腰に民族衣装を巻いて開会式に登場したことが話題となり，一気に有名になりました。2020 年の東京オリンピックにも来るでしょうか？

Surprising Changes in Languages

Languages change differently in different countries. The English in Australia is different from the English in the U.S. The accent is different, and so are some of the words. For example, "Barbie" is a doll in the U.S., but it is a "barbecue" in Australia. Some words are different in the Korean language, too. North and South Korea have been different countries for more than 70 years, and the words have changed in surprising ways. The word for "octopus" in South Korea means "squid" in North Korea. I wonder what the word for "squid" in South Korea means in North Korea.

アメリカ人の大人がほとんど使わない「バービー」という言葉を，オーストラリア人は頻繁に使います。気候のいいオーストラリアでは「バーベキュー」がいつでもできそうですね。北朝鮮から韓国へやってくる人々は戸惑うかもしれません。イカのつもりで食事を頼んだら，タコが出てきてびっくりするでしょう！

Chocolates for Your Teacher

It's Valentine's Day. Who are you going to give chocolate to? Or will you send a heart-shaped card (called a valentine) instead? One American high school student got a B- on a paper that he wrote for class. He wanted to get a better grade, so he sent his teacher some chocolates. They were in a special Valentine's Day box with the traditional message "Be Mine" printed on the top. That means "I want you to be my sweetheart." The next day, the teacher gave him a valentine. When he opened it, he laughed. It said, "Thank you for the chocolates, but your grade is still a Be Mine-us (B-)."

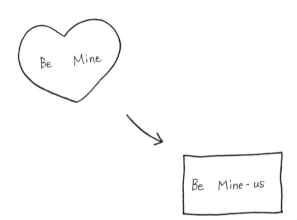

 日本には，バレンタイン・デーに先生にチョコレートをあげる子はいますか？ アメリカにはこのようにごまをする子もいるようです。ただし，先生はそう甘くはありません。チョコをもらっても，成績を変えることはありません。この先生は素晴らしいダジャレで返しました！

Cat Therapy Works!

Someone I know told me about a friend who was suffering from depression. He kept away from people for several years. None of his friends could do anything to help him. Then his psychologist suggested that he keep a cat. He followed the psychologist's advice and went to a pet shop. As soon as he went into the shop, he fell in love with one cat. He decided to buy the cat, and since then, he has been getting better. Now he doesn't suffer from depression and has started to work part-time. Cat therapy seems to have worked.

(Written by a reader, Imai Takao)

depression　うつ病　　psychologist　心理学者，精神科医

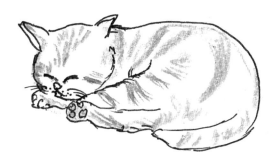

 猫や犬のような，昔からペットとして飼われている
動物との触れ合いは人を癒す効果があります。言葉
がいらず，なでるだけでコミュニケーションが成り
立つので，複雑なことを考えなくてもいいですね。

He Said That He Would

Hanyu Yuzuru gave two great performances at the PyeongChang Winter Olympics and got the gold medal in men's figure skating for the second time in four years. I missed seeing both the short and the free programs because I was on my way to Australia. It was my sister in the U.S. who gave me the news. She wrote a short email that said, "Yuzuru Hanyu frenzy at the Olympics!" I double-checked and found out that Hanyu was the winner. He said that he would get the gold, and he did! Uno Shoma was not far behind. He came in second, giving Japan the silver medal as well.

frenzy　熱狂　　double-check　再確認する

この数年間，羽生結弦選手に勝てる人はなかなかいませんね。彼の強さはスケートの技術だけではありません。負けず嫌いな性格なので，いつも完璧に近い演技ができるように練習して，金メダルを他の選手に譲りません。

Plastic Money and Heavy Coins

Australian money is similar to American money. Both countries use dollars, and each dollar is 100 cents. There are some big differences, however. Australian bills are made of plastic. I don't know if it is true, but someone told me that Australians wanted to make money that would be all right even if they went swimming. Plastic money certainly doesn't show wear like paper bills do! Most Australian coins are round, but the 50-cent coin has 12 sides. It is so big and heavy that you don't want to carry more than one. The 1- and 2-dollar coins are much smaller than the 50-cent coin and are a different color.

show wear　すり切れる

 オーストラリアの紙幣はプラスチックでできているので，ポケットに入れたまま泳ぎに行っても破れません。最先端技術を使って紙幣を作っているオーストラリアですが，なぜか昔ながらの重い 50 セント硬貨を今でも使用しているのは不思議ですね。

Closed until the Chicken Comes

How would you feel if you went to your favorite noodle restaurant and were told that they were closed because they didn't have enough noodles? That is happening in Britain now with chicken. Kentucky Fried Chicken doesn't have enough chicken to make its most famous product, fried chicken. Apparently, KFC changed the company that delivers their chicken. For some reason, the new company is not delivering the chicken. Because there isn't any chicken, stores all over Britain are closing until the chicken comes. People in Britain eat a lot of chicken, so there are lots of disappointed customers.

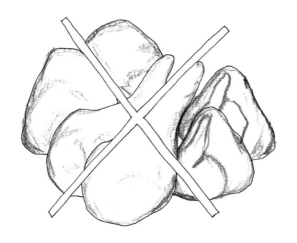

 イギリスのケンタッキーフライドチキンの店が，鶏肉不足で臨時休業になりました。客はもちろんがっかりしていますが，KFC で働くスタッフのほうが大変でしょう。急に仕事がなくなり，しばらく家で待機するしかありません。その間収入がなくて困っているに違いありません。

Australian Wildlife

The wildlife is what makes Australia so different from other countries. No trip should be without a visit to see Australian animals. Yesterday, we saw and heard the famous kookaburra, a bird that sounds like it is laughing, from a steam railway. Then we went to an animal park where we could touch and feed kangaroos, cockatoos (white birds) and emus (big birds that cannot fly). We saw koalas and wombats there, too. Finally, we went to Phillip Island to see penguins come out of the ocean and bring food to their babies. Wallabies (small kangaroos) and geese were eating grass in nearby fields.

wildlife　野生生物　　kookaburra　ワライカワセミ
cockatoo　（ここでは)キバタン

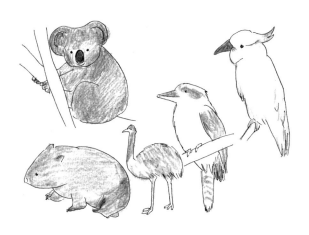

オーストラリアには独特な固有の動物が数多くいますが，簡単に見ることができるのは鳥です。都会にもカササギフエガラスやキバタン（白いオウム），森の中にはワライカワセミやエミュー（ダチョウくらい大きな鳥）がいます。バードウォッチングの好きな僕にとっては天国ですね。

Digital Detox Boot Camp

In Australia, just like in Japan, teenagers have smartphones and are always connected to the Internet. Unfortunately, some of them spend too much time online and cannot make friends. Now there is a nine-day digital detox boot camp where parents can send their teenagers to get them away from technology. Veterans (soldiers with war experience) run the camp. They get the teenagers to exercise, and they take them on adventure activities like sky-diving and hiking. The veterans believe that if the teenagers learn teamwork and feel better about themselves, they can control their use of technology.

detox（detoxification の略）　中毒患者の解毒療法

四六時中，携帯電話を触っている若者が増えています。ゲーム機やパソコンから離れられない子どももたくさんいると思います。寝不足になっても自分ではやめられません。そこで，元軍人が9日間の訓練（boot camp）を通じて，子どもたちを電子機器から離します。

100 Things to Do

On January 1, I made a list of 100 things to do such as "don't complain for a day" and "talk to someone who is lonely." All of them are difficult for me. Yesterday I went shopping in Osaka, and on my way home someone spoke to me. He said that he couldn't find his train. His train left from a different station, but I managed to explain the way to the station. He thanked to me, and I was happy to see his happy face. I remembered that my list included giving directions to a foreigner. I was able to do it! It gave me self-confidence. Now I have a feeling that I can do the other 99 things.

(Written by a reader, Minakata Norika)

1. Don't complain for a day.

2. Talk to someone who is lonely.

3. ...

 この読者の新年の誓いはとても現実的だと思いま
す。色々な1回限りの目標を立てて，1つずつこな
していきます。1回やればいい(続けなくていい)の
で，三日坊主にならなくて済みますね。

A Tour Guide's Story

There was a tour guide who loved trains. He was very happy a few years ago when he had a chance to take a group on the Cassiopeia, an overnight luxury train from Sapporo to Tokyo. The train made a stop in the middle of the night, probably to take on food and drinks. Because it was so late, the train doors opened quietly. The tour guide got off wearing just a sweat shirt and sweat pants and brought his cell phone with him. He went to the front of the train and took a picture. Just then, the doors closed and the train started to move. The guide tried to stop the train by hitting the window with his hands, but it didn't stop. Instead, the police arrested him after seeing him on the station camera. He told them that he had to get back to his group on the train, but they didn't believe him. They called the Cassiopeia, and luckily the conductor said that he was telling the truth. But how did he get back to the train? A police officer took him to Fukushima by Shinkansen. When the Cassiopeia came into the station, he got back on. It was still early in the morning, so no one on the tour ever found out!

take on 〜　〜（荷物など）を積み込む　　arrest　逮捕する
conductor　車掌

この話は他のツアーガイドの人から聞きました。普通は自分の会社では語れない内緒の話だと思いますが，同僚のガイドに明かしたため，僕の耳にも入りました。もし戻れなかったらどうなっていたでしょうか？　でも，お客さんが知らないうちに無事に戻って来られて良かったです。

N Is for ….

On my desk at the office, I have this calendar. Each month has a picture by students from a special needs school. February has a cute illustration titled, "Alphabet Shaped Animals." Colorful animals are shaped into the letters from A to Z. For example, A is for an alligator with a jagged back and S is for a swan with a curvy neck. It is so much fun to find out what they are. I am amazed by their creativity! However, I don't know what N is for. The animal for this letter looks like a snake but has four legs and a long tail. What is it?

(Written by a reader, Ishitobi Noriko)

special needs school　特別支援学校　　alligator　ワニ
jagged　ギザギザの　　curvy　曲がりくねった

動物の絵を使ってアルファベットの形を表すのに感心しました。この読者が，Nの動物がイモリだと分からなかったのは仕方ないでしょう。たまたま僕の好きな映画に出てくる動物なので，僕はすぐに想像できましたが，一般的にはあまり知られていません。

答え It's a newt.

47

A Real Superwoman

Can you believe it? Muraoka Momoka has won four medals at the Paralympics in five days! She won her first medal in the downhill on Saturday. That was a silver. On Sunday, she got the bronze in the Alpine skiing super-G. Then, on Tuesday, she got her third medal in the Alpine skiing super combined. It was another bronze. Yesterday she got her fourth medal. This time, it was gold. It is also the first gold medal for any Japanese athlete at the PyeongChang Paralympics. And she may win another medal before the Paralympics are over!

この記事を書いた時点で，村岡選手は4つのメダルを手にしていましたが，最終日のアルペンスキー女子回転で2位をマークして，さらに銀メダルを獲得しました。平昌パラリンピックで，日本人選手として最多となる5個のメダルを獲得しました。

The Cherry Blossom Season Has Begun

On Friday, I was watching the TV evening news, and there was a reporter at Yasukuni Shrine in Tokyo. The weather bureau sends people to the shrine every day to see if the cherry trees have blossomed. These people look carefully at one particular cherry tree. If there are more than 5 or 6 blossoms open on this tree, they announce that the cherry blossoms in Tokyo have begun to open. On Friday, it was still too early. On Saturday, they went to the shrine again. This time they said that the cherry blossom season had begun.

weather bureau　気象庁

 気象庁の職員が慎重に開花の判断を下すほど，日本人にとって花見は重要ですね。春は外出するのに良い時期です。花見派はフェイスブックやインスタグラムに桜の写真をたくさんアップしますし，花より団子派は食べて飲んで騒ぐことを楽しみます。

Sightseeing at Home

When you live in one place, you seldom go to the sightseeing places in your area. It's only when someone comes to visit you from out of town that you go to see these places. My younger daughter lives in the U.S., and she came back last week for a visit. On Sunday, we went to Nagoya Castle. I hadn't been there for over 10 years. A lot has changed. The city is rebuilding the Hommaru Palace that was destroyed in World War II. It is a beautiful, wooden palace full of golden painted screens. Outside, people dressed up as ninja and samurai guided tourists and posed for photos. I felt like I was in Kyoto, not Nagoya.

名古屋は頑張っています！　名古屋城の敷地では，名古屋おもてなし武将隊がパフォーマンスをしたり，忍者隊が観光客を出迎えたりしています。本丸御殿が復元されたというニュースは聞いていましたが，次女が名古屋に遊びに来なければ見に行かなかったでしょう。

The Nobel Prize for Children's Books

Have you ever heard of Kadono Eiko? She will get the Hans Christian Andersen Award this year. People call this the Nobel Prize for children's books. She has written many children's books, but most people know her because of "Kiki's Delivery Service." It is Kadono's best known book. It's about a girl who is a half-witch. She can ride a broom and has a black cat named Jiji. After she leaves home, she makes a living delivering things on her broom. Kadono has written at least five more books about Kiki. Actually, I have never read any of the books, but I have seen the movie by Miyazaki Hayao.

「魔女の宅急便」を書いた角野栄子さんが国際アンデルセン賞の作家賞を受賞しました。「魔女の宅急便」はアニメ映画になったので知っていますが，角野さんのことはよく知りませんでした。子どもの心をつかめる本は良いですね。そういった作品を読んだ子どもは大人になっても読書を続けるでしょう。

Too Sweet for Me

Yesterday was April Fool's Day. It was also Easter, a day when children are given chocolate eggs. One company decided to celebrate the two days together. Burger King is one of the biggest hamburger chains in the world and is known for its large hamburger called the Whopper. It put up a video on Twitter on Mar. 30, 2018, saying that it had created a new chocolate Whopper. It is made with a chocolate cake bun, a chocolate patty instead of meat, raspberry syrup instead of ketchup, white chocolate rings instead of onions, and vanilla frosting instead of mayonnaise. That's a little too sweet for me.

bun　パン，バンズ　　patty　パティ
raspberry syrup　キイチゴのシロップ

 Chocolate Whopper で検索するとびっくりするで
しょう。ハンバーガーにそっくりです！　もちろん
エイプリルフールのために作られたので，この商品
は存在しません。想像するだけで胃がおかしくなり
そうです。

The Kangaroo Route

How far can you fly on a passenger plane? The new flight from Perth, Australia, to London, England, is one of the longest passenger flights in the world. It is also the first regular non-stop flight from Australia to Europe. Australia has a close relationship with Britain, and Qantas, the Australian airline, started flying the Kangaroo Route to London in 1947. At that time, it took four days and nine stops. Now, the direct 14,498-kilometer flight takes just 17 hours. This is possible because Qantas has a new jet, the Boeing 787. It is lighter than older jets and uses 20% less fuel.

Perth　パース　　　close relationship　親密な関係　　　direct　直行の
fuel　燃料

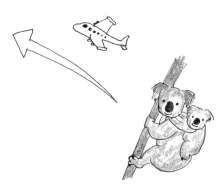

昔は4日かかりましたが，今は1日で着きます！飛行中どのように過ごすかが問題ですが，最近は好きな映画が見放題ですし，本は1冊以上読めるでしょう。ただ，エコノミークラス症候群には気をつけましょう。必ず数回は立って，足を伸ばしたほうが良いと思います。

I Shouldn't Have Doubted Him

Exactly one week ago, I wrote that Ohtani Shohei might have a hard time staying a two-way player. He got a hit in his first game, and then he won his first game as a starting pitcher. He was looking very good, but I didn't think he could keep it up. After I sent out that Jaremaga story, Ohtani hit a home run. In the next game, he hit another home run. He followed that with another home run in his next game. Yesterday, he won his second game, striking out 12 batters in seven innings. I shouldn't have doubted him. He has one of the fastest pitches and is one of the strongest batters in MLB.

doubt　疑う　　two-way player　二刀流の選手

大谷翔平選手は，ベーブ・ルースさん以来初めて二刀流として活躍している選手です。開幕からピッチャーで2勝を挙げ，バッターとしてはホームランを3本も打って，大きな存在感を示しました。

A Regular Worker Wins a Marathon

The Boston Marathon took place on Monday. It was raining with strong winds, and the temperature was only 4 degrees centigrade. In spite of the bad weather, Kawauchi Yuki beat last year's champion and became the first Japanese runner since 1987 to win the Boston Marathon. He is unique among Japanese runners. He isn't a full-time athlete, and he doesn't belong to a team or get sponsorship from companies. He works 40 hours a week for the government of Saitama Prefecture. He is a regular worker who can win marathons! I'm sure we will see him in the Tokyo Olympics.

sponsorship　資金提供

 市民ランナーとして知られていた川内優輝選手が見事にボストン・マラソンで優勝しました。驚いたことに，その後公務員を辞めて，プロとして競技中心の生活を送るようになりました。以前は練習の時間が限られていましたが，これからはランナーとしての可能性を広げるでしょう。

I Know I'm in Japan

At the first meeting of the new school year at my university, the professors were asked to check a list of their names and addresses. One of the new professors raised his hand and said, "The second character in my first name is wrong. I'm sorry." Then we checked another paper. Once again, the same teacher raised his hand and said, "My name is wrong here, too. I'm sorry." I smiled and thought, "I know that I'm in Japan. People say 'I'm sorry' even when someone else makes a mistake."

professor　教授　　character　文字

I'm sorry!

すみません!

 自分が悪くなくても日本人は「すみません」と言います。外国で"I'm sorry."と安易に言うと大変なことになるかもしれません。"I'm sorry."は自分の間違った行為，または正しくない行為を認める場合にのみ使いましょう。

Digging Bamboo Shoots

I look forward to digging bamboo shoots every year. A big park named Makinogaike Park is near my house. The park allows us to dig bamboo shoots for just one week in the spring. There are good bamboo shoots under the ground. The ones that have already come up are not so good. They taste bitter. I have to use not only my eyes but also my hands to find the better ones. I crawl on the ground and stroke the surface with my hands. I search for the tips of the bamboo shoots. As soon as I find one, I dig it up and boil it with rice bran.

(Written by a reader, Manabe Yuko)

dig 掘る　　bamboo shoot　タケノコ　　bitter　苦い
crawl　はう　　rice bran　米ぬか

 公園にタケノコを掘りに行けるのはいいですね。この読者によると，タケノコの先端が地面から出ているものはおいしくないので，地面に手を当てて，まだ土の中に隠れているタケノコを探すそうです。

Why Not the Same Character?

I teach my granddaughter English, and she has started to teach me Japanese. Actually she gives me a Chinese character test each week. Last week, I had to write the correct character for "measure." The pronunciation is "hakaru," but there were three different ways to write it. When you measure how tall someone is, you use one character. When you measure how long it takes to run 100 meters, you use a different character. When you measure how much something weighs, you use one more character. If the pronunciation and the meaning are the same, why can't you use the same character?

Chinese character　漢字

測る

計る

HAKARU?

量る

測る？　計る？　量る？　この3つの漢字はすべて
「はかる」と読みます。意味もよく似ているのに，な
ぜ1つの漢字または平仮名で書かないのでしょう？
日本語の読み書きは本当に難しいと思います！

The Most Dangerous Animal?

What is the most dangerous animal? That depends on the country you are in. New Zealand has hardly any dangerous animals. Australia, on the other hand, has dangerous snakes, spiders, crocodiles, sharks, and even octopuses. My first question is:

(1) Which animal kills the most people in North America?

a. the scorpion b. the deer c. the alligator

(2) Which animal kills the most people in Japan?

a. the viper b. the bear c. the giant hornet

(3) Which animal kills the most people in Africa?

a. the lion b. the hyena c. the hippopotamus

scorpion　サソリ　　viper　マムシ　　giant hornet　オオスズメバチ
hippopotamus　カバ

 毒を持っている動物や大型の肉食動物が一番危険だというイメージを持っている人は多くいると思いますが，必ずしもそうではないことがこのクイズの解答で分かります。意外な動物が人間にとって危ないですね。

(1) b About 200 people are killed each year in traffic accidents with deer.
(2) c The giant hornet kills about 40 people a year in Japan with its sting.
(3) c Almost 3,000 people die each year when they are attacked by hippopotamuses.

答え

The End of Heisei

Emperor Akihito, the Japanese Emperor, plans to step down on April 30, 2019. Japan will have a new emperor at this time next year, and we will say goodbye to Heisei. What will the next era be called? We won't know until next year. Emperor Akihito is not the first emperor to step down. He is the 125th Emperor in a line that goes back to Emperor Jimmu, who was the first Emperor from 660 BC to 585 BC. Emperor Kokaku, the 119th Emperor, also stepped down, but that was about 200 years ago. Emperor Akihito's son, Crown Prince Naruhito, will become the next Emperor of Japan.

step down　退位する

昭和天皇が崩御されたとき，元号を新しくするか，元号を廃止して西暦に統一するかという論争が大きく取り上げられましたが，平成から令和に替わる時にはこの論争はあまり見かけませんでした。伝統を守ることは大切ですが，役所などでは書類の訂正でしわ寄せが来ているように思います。

Parkour and Freerunning

Have you ever heard of parkour and freerunning? They are similar, but freerunning uses more fancy moves than parkour. Runners run and jump over low walls. They spin and they flip. They run along the side of walls for a few steps, or they run up to the top of a wall. When they jump down from a high place, they roll on the ground. They have great balance and skill. This kind of running looks cool, but it can be dangerous. People who make a mistake can break their bones, so they have to practice until they can do each move perfectly.

parkour　パルクール　　fancy　派手な　　flip　宙返りする

若者は安全を考えずに行動する傾向があります。スリルを求めて「フリーランニング」に挑戦する人が増えています。走りながらアクロバットをするこの新しいスポーツは確かに格好良く見えます。

Accepted by 113 Colleges!

U.S. high school students apply to college by February of their last year, and the colleges tell them whether they got in or not by the end of April. Most students apply to fewer than 10 colleges, but one high school girl in North Carolina applied to 115 colleges. She is a great student, so she was accepted by 113 colleges. Not only was she accepted, but she got scholarships from many of these colleges! Which college did she pick? In the end, she decided to go to a college near her hometown. She got a full scholarship, so she doesn't have to pay anything.

apply to ～　～に出願する　　scholarship　奨学金

 アメリカでは，出願費用の安さとインターネットの
おかげで，簡単に複数の大学に出願できますが，こ
の高校生は特別です。113校から合格通知が来まし
たが，結局彼女は姉が通っていた地元の大学に入学
することにしました。

Water and Frogs

I was in a small village in Gifu Prefecture with first-year university students from Monday through Wednesday. The trees around us were beautiful shades of green, and the rice paddies had water in them. They were like mirrors; we could see the mountains in them. It rained every day, so the river was full of water. We went to bed to the sound of water and frogs. One of the students caught a frog. She showed me where they were, and I caught two. One was small and brown with dark stripes, and the other was bright green and even smaller. How can something that small make so much noise?

shade　色合い　　rice paddy　田んぼ

 春先に田舎へ行くと，田んぼの水面に景色が鏡のように映っています。田んぼの中をのぞくと泳いでいるオタマジャクシが見つかります。カエルの声は聞こえますが，簡単には見つかりません。あぜ道の斜面にいるという情報を学生から得て探すと，何匹か捕まえることができました。

Rock, Scissors, Paper

"Rock, scissors, paper" is a great way to choose people. My students use it all the time in class when I ask for volunteers. Did you know that this game comes from Japan? It isn't well known in North America or Europe. I had never heard of it before I came to Japan. So how do people in those countries choose people? One of the most common ways is to flip a coin and guess which side it lands on. However, children usually say this counting poem and point. "Eeny, meeny, miny, moe, catch a tiger by the toe. If he hollers, let him go, eeny, meeny, miny, moe." The person who comes 16th is chosen.

flip a coin　コインを投げる　　holler　叫ぶ

人を選ぶのにジャンケンはとても便利ですね。英語圏にはこんな便利な選び方がないので，子どもは詩を言いながら選びますが，中学生以上になると子どもっぽい詩を言いたくなくて，自分から進んでやることが多くなります。

The Big Winner

Koreeda Hirokazu was the big winner at the 2018 Cannes Film Festival. On May 19, 2018, his film "Shoplifters" won the Palme d'Or, the prize for the best movie. Like most of his other movies, this movie is about a family. This time, however, the family is poor but kind. They find an abused girl and take care of her. Koreeda has been making movies since the 1990s, but I have only seen one other movie by him. I was impressed by the story and the acting. Koreeda is an unusual director. He doesn't just direct his movies. He writes the story and edits the movie, too.

"Shoplifters" 「万引き家族」　abused　虐待された
edit　編集する

 是枝監督の「万引き家族」がカンヌ国際映画祭で最高賞のパルムドールを受賞しました。僕がこの監督を知ったのは「歩いても　歩いても」という映画を友達に勧められて見た時でした。家族をテーマにした,人間味のある良い映画でした。

The First Japanese in Brazil

The largest group of ethnic Japanese outside Japan live in Brazil, and this year they are celebrating the 110th anniversary of their arrival in Brazil. In 1908, a group of Japanese looking for a better life traveled from Kobe to Brazil on the Kasato Maru. When they arrived, most of them went to São Paulo and started to work on coffee farms. They had to work long hours in Brazil, and the pay was not good. Even so, around 250,000 Japanese moved to Brazil. At first, they were poor, but when they got some money, many bought land and started their own farms.

ethnic Japanese　日系人

110
ANOS DA IMIGRAÇÃO
JAPONESA NO BRASIL
ブラジル日本移民百十周年

日系ブラジル人の歴史は意外に長いですね。彼らは
当時の日本での貧しい生活から抜け出したくて，夢
を抱いてブラジルへ渡りました。代々苦労をしてき
ましたが，今ではブラジルで成功している日系人は
少なくありません。

Strange Laws in the U.S.

There are some very strange old laws in the U.S. For example, it's illegal (against the law) to drive blindfolded in Alabama. (Of course! If your eyes are covered, you can't see! Do you need a law to stop people from doing it?) In Arizona, it's illegal for a donkey to sleep in a bathtub. (But why would a donkey sleep in a bathtub? And why is that bad?) In Hawaii, it's illegal to put a coin in your ear. (Are they worried that coins would hurt your ear?) In Montana, it's illegal to raise rats. (Scientists use rats for experiments. Aren't there any scientists in Montana?)

blindfold　目隠しをする

アメリカには昔に制定された訳が分からない法律があります。調べてみると，変な法律があるのはアメリカだけではありません。カナダ・トロント市のある大通りでは，日曜日に馬の死体を引きずる行為が禁じられています。日本では，郵便ポストにアイスクリームを入れることは違法行為とみなされます。

Growing up in Hokkaido

My two sons grew up in a small town in Hokkaido in beautiful natural surroundings. Their father took them wherever they wanted to go to play. In summer, they caught a lot of tadpoles. After a while, the tadpoles became frogs, and we let them go. In winter, we went skiing and skating. That's why they like nature. My older son still enjoys climbing and backcountry skiing. My second son keeps newts as pets. He says that the way they move is cute. I think that my sons' childhood experiences have led to their current lifestyles.

(Written by a reader, Watanabe Seiko)

natural surroundings   自然環境   tadpole   オタマジャクシ

この話にあるように，育てられた環境は人生に大きな影響を与えます。大人になっても住んでいる環境によって人が変わることはあるでしょう。運動嫌いだった僕の次女は，大人になってからスポーツが好きになり，今ではボルダリングに一生懸命です。親はびっくりです！

From the Size of Their Waists

When I ride my bicycle to the university, I go near a high school. In the morning, the streets are filled with boys and girls. Last Friday was June 1, 2018, and all the boys were wearing black trousers and short-sleeved white shirts. I realized that it was the first day of summer (at least for summer clothes). On my way back home, I was riding along the main street near the high school, and I passed a group of men wearing black trousers and short-sleeved white shirts. How could I tell that they were men and not boys? Not from their clothes. I could tell from the size of their waists!

 この高校の男子生徒の夏の制服はサラリーマンの服装と妙に似ています。白いワイシャツに黒いズボンは共通です。ただし、サラリーマンは中年太りなので後ろ姿でも見分けられます。女子の制服と大人の服はあまりにも違うので、見間違えることはありません。

Speak of the Devil

The weather was great last Sunday, and I went for a walk beside the Shonai River with some other birdwatchers. I had done this walk several times before, but I had never seen a striated heron. The people I was with were surprised because this is a good place to see this bird. They told me that many birdwatchers came to Fujimae Tidal Flat from Osaka just to take pictures of striated herons. Well, speak of the devil! There was a striated heron on some rocks in the river. I got within 20 meters of the bird and took more than 50 pictures!

speak of the devil　うわさをすれば影　　striated heron　ササゴイ

バードウォッチングは自然の中で行われるので，自由に動き回る生きものを見つけられる保証はありません。今回はラッキーでした。ササゴイが川にある石の上に立って一生懸命，餌を取っていました。撮った写真をプロ並みと言われて，うれしかったです。

Now Women Can Drive

Saudi Arabia is a very rich country. The capital, Riyadh, has many tall buildings and wide streets, but there is hardly any public transportation. If you work, you need to go to the office by car. Saudi Arabia is the place where Islam began. For many years, women could not get driver's licenses in Saudi Arabia because some powerful leaders of Islam in that country made strict rules for women. If a woman wanted to go somewhere, she had to find a man to drive her. Now, the country has changed its rules. As of June this year, women can get a driver's license and drive a car.

public transportation　公共交通機関　　Islam　イスラム教

イスラム教の発祥の地であるサウジアラビアでは，政府は保守的な考えを重視してきましたが，最近変わりつつあります。女性の社会進出を事実上承認するようになってきました。働く女性の増加に伴い，規制を少しずつ緩和するようになりました。

Not the First Time

I went to see students who were doing teaching practice outside Nagoya. I fell asleep on the train back, and when I opened my eyes, my train was coming into Kariyashi. I had to change from one train line to another at Kariya. A lot of people were on the platform, so I got off. When I got to the exit, I realized that I was at the wrong station. I was told that Kariya was the next stop after Kariyashi. I had to wait another 15 minutes for the next train. Why are there two stations with almost the same name next to each other? I'm sure this isn't the first time someone has made this mistake.

 名古屋鉄道では「刈谷」という駅の隣に「刈谷市」という駅があります。ややこしいと思いませんか？　せめて西にある「刈谷市」を「西刈谷」に改名すべきだと思います。「刈谷市」で間違えて降りた乗客は数えきれないほどいると思います。

Will I Lose My Job?

A few schools in Japan have started to use special robots in their classes. Children can talk to them in English. These robots are different from voice recognition software on a mobile phone like Siri. Siri can answer your questions, but it can't have a conversation. It can tell you what its favorite movie is, but it cannot tell you why it likes the movie. One small robot called Musio can tell you why it likes something. It can see, so if you show it something, it can tell you what it is. It learns and remembers things. Will robots become English teachers? Will I lose my job? Not yet, I hope!

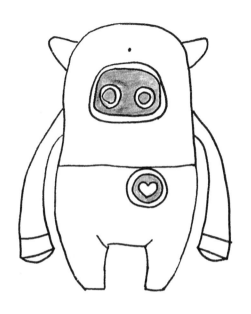

英語学習には AI が有効かもしれません。AI なら朝早くても「起こしたら悪い」と遠慮する必要がありません。人間のように学ぶ力があるので，色々な発言ができるようになります。しかし，ずっとロボットと話したいという人はどれだけいるでしょうか？人間の英語教師はまだまだロボットには負けないと僕は思います。

"Shoplifters"

I went to see the new movie by Koreeda Hirokazu last Sunday. It's called "Manbiki Kazoku" or "Shoplifters" in English. I understand why it won first prize at the Cannes Film Festival. The story is very powerful. It's about a very unusual family. They live together in an old house and help each other. They do things that are wrong, but everyone is full of love. There isn't a lot of action in the movie, and there is hardly any music. Even so, I'm glad that I saw it at a movie theater. The movie kept me wondering what was going to happen, and the ending was a surprise.

最近はインターネットを使って映画を見ることが多くなりました。今回は妻と一緒に映画館で見てきました。映画館で見ると，すべてを忘れて映画の世界に没頭できます。2人とも感動して帰ってきました。

Bird Rescue

I helped to rescue a large bird called a grey heron. Grey herons usually stay near water and catch fish, but someone found this bird at a parking lot in the city. It was very weak and too tired to fly away. We used a large net to catch it. We didn't have a place to keep the bird, and it wasn't hurt, so we released it at the tidal flat. I watched it every day, but it never got stronger. One day, I saw a boy chasing it, but the bird still couldn't fly. It just walked away. Unfortunately, it died after a few days. If I had rescued the bird sooner, I think it would still be alive.

(Written by a reader, Manabe Yuko)

rescue 救助(する)　grey heron アオサギ　release 放つ

この読者は稲永ビジターセンターに勤務しています。ある日，彼女はアオサギを救助できないかという電話を受けて，他の専門家と一緒に現地へ捕まえに行きました。アオサギの体長は約1メートルありますが，弱っていたため簡単に捕まえることができました。

How Do You Pay?

When you go to a store or a restaurant, how do you pay? Do you use cash, do you pay by credit card, or do you use a prepaid card? According to one magazine, most people in Japan still use cash for their purchases. Only 18% of purchases are made without using cash. In China, things are different. Sixty percent of purchases are cashless. How do so many people in China shop without cash? They use their cell phones and pay just by scanning a QR code. LINE, Japan's biggest chat app operator, has a similar cashless payment system. I'm sure that it will change the way people pay in Japan.

purchase　買い物　　cashless　現金不要の

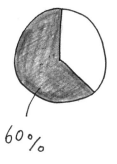

60%

日本ではキャッシュレス決済はそれほど普及していませんが，現在中国では約60％の決済がキャッシュレスで行われています。世界でキャッシュレス社会に一番乗りする国は，おそらく北欧のスウェーデンでしょう。2023年までに完全キャッシュレス化を目指しています。

Wishes

It's two days before *Tanabata*. At my university, they put up bamboo branches in front of one building. There are colored paper strips on a table, so students can write their wishes and hang the strips on the bamboo. I read some of the wishes yesterday. Many students wanted to meet a famous TV personality or go to a concert. One of them said that she wanted to get married before she turned 25. I expected to see a lot of wishes about passing the teacher recruitment examination. Most of my students want to become elementary school teachers and have to take it soon. Surprisingly, I only found one.

teacher recruitment examination　教員採用試験

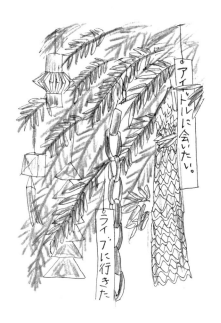

アイドルに会いたい。

ライブに行きた

人前で自分の願い事をはっきり言える人は少ないと
思いますが，このような公の場で願い事を書いて吊
るすのは平気ですね。たくさんある中なら，怖くな
くて，解放された気分になるでしょう。

July 9, 2018

Germany in Nagoya

The Oktoberfest is a beer festival that takes place in Germany in the autumn. Nagoya has its own Oktoberfest, but it is in July. This year's festival began last Friday, so my wife and I decided to go there after dinner on Saturday. When we got there, it was raining. There were stalls selling beer and sausages, but not many customers were sitting at the tables under tents. I suddenly heard my name. Some students from my university were working there part-time! We bought some sausages and beer and sat down. The food and beer were delicious. We enjoyed that night in spite of the weather.

stall　屋台

夕食後にオクトーバーフェストを訪れたため満腹に近い状態でした。僕の大学の学生に誘われなかったら何も買わなかったでしょう。僕の祖母はオーストリア出身で，その影響で僕はドイツ圏のビールとソーセージが大好きです。値段は高かったですが，懐かしい味でした。

A Great Rescue

A coach and 12 boys on a local soccer team went missing in northern Thailand on June 23. They went into a cave, but a sudden rain came and quickly filled part of the cave with water. Many countries sent help, and the team was found 9 days later by two British divers. The boys were hungry but healthy. The problem was how to get them out. The cave was dark and very narrow in some places, and the boys couldn't swim. One Thai diver died trying to rescue them, but the other divers were able to bring the boys out four at a time. The last boys came out yesterday. What a rescue!

go missing　行方不明になる　　cave　洞窟

昔はなかなか耳に入らなかった外国のニュースが，最近は全世界で報道されるようになり，さまざまな国から援助が来るようになりました。国際協力のおかげで少年サッカーチームは助かりました。

The Rainy Season Ends and the Cicadas Begin

The rainy season has ended in Nagoya, and it's time for the cicadas. I can hear them in the morning when I go to work. From my house, I can hear the ones that live in the trees at a nearby university. Are cicadas the loudest insects in the world? According to an article by the BBC, some are. There are many kinds of cicadas around the world, and scientists have measured their calls. Some cicadas have calls louder than 100 decibels! Cicadas in Japan are not that loud, but they have calls that are 70-90 decibels. When I walk through a park full of trees, the noise is incredible.

cicada セミ   incredible すごい

アメリカには周期ゼミがいて，13 年または 17 年お
きに大量発生するので，アメリカ人にとってセミは
あまり身近な存在ではありません。日本では毎年ど
こでもセミの声が聞こえてくるので，夏＝セミのイ
メージです。森に入ると耳が痛くなるほどうるさい
虫です。

And the Winner Is ….

The FIFA World Cup final is over. The match was between Croatia, a country of just over 4 million, and France, a country of almost 70 million. I was impressed by Croatia because the players never gave up. France was ahead 2-1 at the end of the first half, but Croatia was looking good. They had the ball more and kept on shooting. In the second half, France got two goals, one after the other, and the score was 4-1. It looked like the game was over, but Croatia scored against the French goalee. The score was now 4-2. Could Croatia win? In the end, they lost to France, 4-2, but they did a great job!

look good　調子が良さそうに見える　　goalee　ゴールキーパー

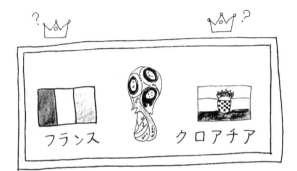

 サッカーワールドカップの優勝国はフランスになり
ましたが，クロアチアという人口の少ない国に，フ
ランスを相手にできるほどの力があることはすごい
ですね！　負けていても最後まで頑張る選手を見る
と元気が出ます。

Why Do Names Change?

Why do the names of places change? Last weekend, I was watching a TV program with the comedian Tamori. He visited Shimonoseki and Moji in southern Japan to find out why the name of the water between the two cities changed from the Straits of Shimonoseki to the Kanmon Straits in the Meiji Era. Shimonoseki was a famous place in the Edo Period for fish, but in the Meiji Period, Moji quickly grew rich because it was the port for Kyushu's coal. The new name of the straits came from the last character of Shimonoseki and the first character of Moji. It showed that both cities were important.

strait(s) 海峡　　coal 石炭　　character 漢字

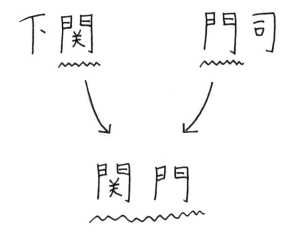

 地名が変わった例はたくさんありますが，なぜ変わったのかは興味深いですね。日本で江戸を東京に改名したのはなぜでしょうか？　ソ連が崩壊してロシアなどの国々に分裂したとき，レニングラードからロシア革命前の名前であるサンクトペテルブルクに戻したのはなぜでしょうか？

Not Enough Ninja

According to a story on the Internet, Japan doesn't have enough ninja. Iga, hometown of the ninja, needs more ninja, and ninja can make 9,000,000 yen a year. People from other countries have read the story and are excited. They love ninja and are sending emails to the city because they want a job. The only problem is that this story is not true. When an American reporter visited Iga, the mayor told her that the city wanted to attract more tourists with its ninja shows and museum. He never said that the city needed ninja. Now he wants people to stop sending emails to the city.

mayor　市長　　attract tourists　観光客を呼び込む

このようなデマによって伊賀市役所は大忙し！
笑っている場合ではありません。インターネット上
の情報は必ずしも正しいとは限りません。注意して
読まないと本当かどうかは分かりません。情報源を
確認してから判断すると良いでしょう。

Japan's Coolest Dessert

It's summer, and it's hot. This is the season for Japan's coolest dessert: shaved ice. In my neighborhood, there is a store that used to sell ice. The husband delivered ice all year round, and the wife sold shaved ice in the summer. Now the store is run by the daughter, and it is only open in summer. They no longer sell ice. Instead, they put tables and stools outside and sell shaved ice to the customers. I like the place because there is no air conditioning. We can sit by the side of the street and watch the cars go by. I want to be hot when I eat shaved ice.

stool　丸椅子

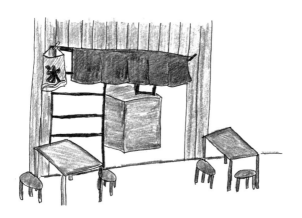

 かき氷を店の前のテーブルに座って食べると，夏の
蒸し暑さが吹き飛びます。僕は宇治金時が一番好き
です。早く夏が来ないかな。また食べたいです。

Ice Cream Quiz

Ice cream is one of the world's most popular desserts. How much do you know about it?

(1) What is the most popular ice cream flavor?

(2) Where was the first ice cream made?

(3) How did people make ice cream before there were freezers?

(4) When was the ice cream cone first made?

(5) How do they sell ice cream to children in summer in the U.S. and Britain?

freezer 冷凍庫

夏に食べたくなるアイスクリームですが，冷凍庫がない時代，作るのに欠かせないものは何だったでしょうか。それは氷でした。冬に池の表面に張った氷を大きなブロックに切り，夏まで氷室で眠らせました。氷は干し草で包んで保管され，夏になるとアイスクリーム作りに使われました。

(1) It depends on the country. In the U.S., it's mint chocolate chip. In Japan, it's vanilla.

(2) The first iced dessert with milk was probably created in China 4,000 years ago.

(3) They mixed cream, sugar and flavorings in a bowl over ice until it was frozen.

(4) In the U.S. around 1900.

(5) There are ice cream trucks that come to your neighborhood.

答え

Something New

Last Thursday I was a guide for a young American man and his uncle. The uncle is a friend who lives in the area, but he doesn't drive. I decided to take them up Mt. Ibuki to escape the heat. The temperature was much cooler. Then we went on to see Hikone Castle, one of Japan's 12 original castles. I smiled at the first picture he took. It was inside the castle museum, but it wasn't something old and valuable. He wanted to remember Japan by the differences in culture, so he took a picture of the slippers on the shelf. Changing into slippers when you go into a building was something new to him.

Mt. Ibuki　伊吹山　　escape the heat　暑さから逃れる

 欧米では，建物の中に入る時に靴を脱ぐ習慣があり
ません。下駄箱そのものが存在しないので，頭の高
さまでスリッパがたくさん入っている下駄箱は，ア
メリカ人にとって不思議な光景に見えるでしょう。

TOPIK

I took a Korean proficiency test in the middle of July, and I remembered that I could check my score online. When I got home last Friday, I turned on my computer and went to the testing site. I was a little worried because the reading part was challenging, but I passed. My listening score was very good, and my reading score was almost 75%. This test was good for me because it made me read every day. I knew that I couldn't pass the test without good reading skills. By the way, do any readers of Jaremaga take English tests? If so, which ones do you take? Do the tests make you study harder?

TOPIK　韓国語能力試験 (= Test of Proficiency in Korean)
proficiency　熟達，運用能力

英検準1級の合格を目指している英語教員の読者からメールが来ました。勉強はしているが試験勉強はつまらなくて勉強意欲がわかないと書いてありました。試験は個人の好みに合わせてはくれないので，残念ながら興味のない話題も勉強しなければ合格できないでしょう。

Taking English Tests

Many readers said that they took the EIKEN. One reader passed the first part in high school but couldn't take the second speaking test because it was on the day of his school trip. Now, many years later, he is looking forward to taking it again, this time with his two teenage daughters. For some people, the listening section is more difficult. For others, the reading part is harder. A couple of teachers said that they needed to take the test for their jobs. One teacher said that it keeps her studying English. However, another teacher said that just studying for a test isn't very motivating.

 読者から寄せられたメールを見る限り，ほとんどの人が英検を受けています。TOEICを受ける人もたくさんいますが，「ビジネス英語」をベースにした試験なので，高校生や教員は内容を難しく感じるかもしれません。

A Street Sign to Your House?

What do you do when people cannot find your house? Usually people just attach a map to an email or send a link to a google map. Someone in a small city in California had a different idea. He probably wanted to help delivery truck drivers find his house, so he put up a sign on a road under two other real signs. It said "Bob's House" and had an arrow pointing to the right. It was dark green with white letters, just like the real signs. The city officials were not angry. They had a good laugh, but they had to take the sign down. They are keeping it in case Bob wants to come and take it home.

attach　添付する　　delivery truck　配達用トラック
take 〜 down　〜を取り外す

写真を見ると，本物の道路標識にそっくりです。役所の人たちは怒るどころか，発想が面白いと笑ったそうです。看板は丁寧に作ったボブのために取っておき，本人が現れたら返すそうです。

Delivered to Your Umbrella

I spent yesterday morning with my wife at a beach in Pusan. Even though it is one of Korea's largest cities, it has the longest beach in the country. Both my wife and I love to swim, so this is where we decided to start our vacation. We rented a beach umbrella and stayed the whole morning. In Korea, you don't have to take a picnic lunch because people come around and drop menus onto your blanket. Fried chicken is the most common food on the menu, but you can order anything from noodles to fried pork. They will deliver it to your umbrella.

Pusan　釜山(プサン)

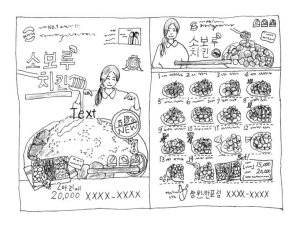

 韓国では食べ物の配達が盛んで，どこからでも注文ができます。韓国映画のワンシーンでは，配達する男性をいじめるために田んぼの中から注文した意地悪な刑事がいました。食べ物の配達を一回は試してみたいと思いますが，このときは観光で来ていたので，昼食はレストランで美味しいものを食べました。

Goodbye, Aretha Franklin

A great American singer died last week. Aretha Franklin passed away at the age of 76. I remember hearing my first Aretha Franklin song in the 1960s when I was a high school student. That was a great time for American music because black musicians like Ray Charles, Aretha Franklin and Stevie Wonder were bringing new sounds into pop music. Aretha started as a gospel singer in her father's church, but she decided to become a professional singer. During her career, she won 18 Grammy Awards and had many hits, but I still think her best song is "Respect," the song I first remember her singing.

pass away 亡くなる　gospel　ゴスペル
Grammy Award　グラミー賞

 60年代のアメリカのポップ音楽には，黒人アーティストの大きな影響がありました。ラジオでは僕の大好きな3人（レイ・チャールズさん，アレサ・フランクリンさん，スティーヴィー・ワンダーさん）のうち，だれかのヒット曲が必ず流れていました。アレサさんの「Respect」はアメリカ人女性の間で大きな反響を呼びました。

It Ended with a Rainbow

Yesterday the drama of Koshien came to an end. The final result was so important that the newscasters talked about it at the beginning of the TV news instead of at the end with the other sports programs. I found highlights on YouTube and watched as Osaka Toin High School kept scoring. In the end, Kanaashi Agricultural High School did not become the first team from Tohoku to win. Instead, Osaka Toin won both the spring and summer tournaments. Even nature was watching this game. It ended with a rainbow.

drama　劇的な出来事

大阪桐蔭 優勝										

金足農	0	0	1	0	0	0	1	0	0	2
大阪桐蔭	3	0	0	3	6	0	1	0	X	13

○○新聞
8月21日

金足農を破り 春夏連覇

号外

2018年の夏，僕は珍しくアメリカへ帰らずに日本にいました。久しぶりに関心を持って夏の甲子園のニュースを毎日見ていました。なぜいつもこんなに劇的な決勝戦になるのでしょうか？ すごく感動しました！ 2018年のドラフトで，大阪桐蔭のスターである根尾選手がドラゴンズに入団することが決定しました。

What Is a Sport?

What is a sport? Can a card game be a sport? This year's Asian Games include one card game called "contract bridge." The Asian Games website says, "Bridge is a card game which is played by four players. This sport is new in the Asian Games." This is the first time I have heard someone call a card game a sport. Contract bridge is not well known in Japan, but it is a very popular game in Europe and North America. You don't need to be physically active to play it, but you need to be mentally active. If contract bridge is a sport, what about video games? Or mah-jong? Or shogi? Or go? Or even Othello?

(the) Asian Games　アジア競技大会
physically active　体をよく動かす　　mentally active　頭をよく使う
mah-jong　麻雀　　go　囲碁

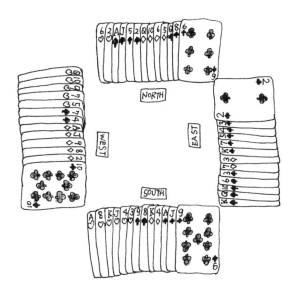

スポーツの定義を調べてみると「身体運動」の要素が必ず入っています。多くのスポーツもゲームも競争の要素が含まれますが、身体運動のほとんどないブリッジがスポーツであるという考え方は僕には理解し難いです。

Ikee Rikako, MVP

The 18th Asian Games have come to an end. China, Japan and Korea were the three big winners, but Indonesia, the host country, came in fourth with a total of 98 medals. Japan got one gold medal on the last day for the mixed relay triathlon. That brought their total to 75 golds. There were many great performances, but Ikee Rikako's was the best. She was chosen as the Most Valuable Player (MVP) for her six gold medals and two silver medals in swimming. She is the first female athlete to receive the MVP award in the Asian Games.

オリンピックではありませんでしたが，池江璃花子
選手がアメリカのマイケル・フェルプスさんのよう
に，金メダルを数多く取りました。彼女は2019年
2月に白血病と診断されたことを公表し，現在治療
中です。病気が早く治って競技に復帰できますよう
に！

Jingisukan

I had *jingisukan* with my friend in Asahikawa. He introduced me to this grilled meat dish many years ago. The name comes from Genghis Khan, the great Mongolian king. It is said that Mongolian soldiers used to cook meat on their helmets, so the metal pan is dome-shaped. Actually, it is good for cooking mutton because the fat runs down to the bottom and the meat doesn't taste so greasy. I first had *jingisukan* when my friend brought some back from Asahikawa. The mutton used to be marinated, but these days, people seem to prefer grilling unseasoned meat and then dipping it in a sauce.

Genghis Khan　ジンギス・カン(チンギス・ハン)　　soldier　兵士
mutton　羊肉　　greasy　脂っこい　　marinate　(タレに)漬け込む
unseasoned　味つけされていない

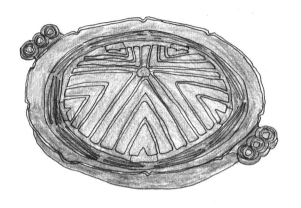

 初めてジンギスカン鍋を見た時，とても印象に残り
ました。まさにかぶとの形をしていました。普通の
鍋と違って，表面に刻まれた溝のおかげで溶けた脂
が流れるので，肉が脂っぽくなくておいしいです。

Goodbye to a Nagoya Symbol

The Chunichi Building will be torn down. It has been a symbol of downtown Nagoya since it was built in 1966. It had Nagoya's only revolving restaurant and one of Nagoya's two theaters for kabuki and musicals. Now the restaurant and the theater are closed, but the beer garden on the roof is still open. Last night, I went to the top of the building with a group of people who study tap dance. I hadn't been to a beer garden in many years. Was I surprised! Of course they had beer and salty food, but they had many other drinks and healthy food, too. They even had desserts!

be torn down　取り壊される
revolving restaurant　回転レストラン

ビアガーデンが進化していて，豊富な種類の飲み物や食べ物が並べられているのに驚きました。2019年になって中日ビルが閉館し，今度はどういうビルになるのか楽しみにしています。

A Star-Filled Night

A terrible earthquake hit Hokkaido on September 6. I felt very sorry for the people there. Actually, my daughter and her family live in Furano. The earthquake there registered 4 on the Japanese scale. I was very worried about them because they have little children. There was a blackout, so they didn't have any electricity. Finally, I got a call from her. Fortunately, nothing was damaged, and everyone was safe. She said that the family enjoyed watching the stars during the blackout. She had never seen such a stunning star-filled sky! I was surprised at how positive they were about it.

(Written by a reader, Bando Shinko)

register ～ on the Japanese scale 震度～を記録する
blackout 停電   stunning 驚くほど美しい

 平成30年9月6日の地震で北海道全域に停電が発生しました。この家族が住んでいる富良野市では震度4を観測しましたが，大きな被害はありませんでした。そのため，いくらか心の余裕があったのか，停電で光がまったくない夜に外で星空を楽しんだそうです。

Greying Japan

Today is Respect for the Aged Day. This is the day to say "hello" and "thank you" to your grandmother or grandfather. Don't forget to be nice to the other elderly people in your neighborhood, too. When this holiday was created in 1966, there were about 6 million people who were elderly (65 and over). About 250 of them were 100 years old and older. Now there are more than 35 million elderly people in Japan. They make up almost 28% of Japan's population. About 70,000 of them are 100 years and older. Japan is definitely greying!

greying　高齢化する　　Respect for the Aged Day　敬老の日
elderly　高齢の

人口の高齢化に伴い，高齢者の中で2つの区分ができました。「前期高齢者」は65歳～74歳，「後期高齢者」は75歳以上の人です。この比較的若い前期高齢者は，社会での活躍を期待されるようになるでしょう。

Shopping Spree

The other day I went to two bookstores with another professor from my university. Our job was to choose English books for the university. It reminded me of an old American TV program called "Supermarket Sweep." On that show, three husband-and-wife teams went on a shopping spree. They raced through a supermarket and put as many things as they could in a shopping cart within a time limit. The team with the largest shopping bill won the game, but everyone took the things in their carts home. My colleague and I didn't race, but we bought a lot of books. Both of us had a great time!

shopping spree　買い物をしまくること，爆買い
within a time limit　制限時間内に　　　bill　勘定

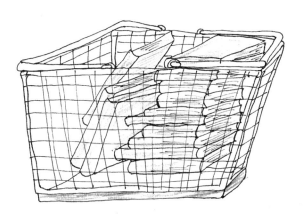

 僕の口ぐせは「買い物は好きじゃない」ですが，本は別です。スーパーで買い物するテレビ番組に出たいと思ったことはありませんが，本屋さんだったらいつでも参加します。でも，もし僕がたくさん本を持って帰ったら，妻が渋い顔をするのが目に浮かびます。「置く場所がないんじゃない？」と言いそうです。

Never Again!

An 18-year-old man in Indonesia was working as a fisherman. He was living alone out at sea on a *rompong*, a very small boathouse. In the middle of July, the rope to the anchor broke, and his *rompong* drifted away. He ran out of food and water after one week. How did he survive? He caught fish and ate them, and he drank rainwater. A ship finally picked him up near Guam, almost 2,000 kilometers from his home, on August 31. He was taken to Japan, and he flew back home to Indonesia. He was happy to be home, but he said that he would never live and work on a *rompong* again!

anchor　いかり　　run out of ～　～を切らす，～がなくなる
survive　生き延びる

インドネシアにこのような漁法があるとは知りませんでした。1人でロンポンといういかだに乗り込み，魚をおびき寄せる仕事で，週に1度食料などを届けてくれる人にしか会うことのない最もさみしい仕事の1つです。49日間も流されて，二度とロンポンに戻らないと決めたこの男性の気持ちはよく分かります。

The Same Architect

I met Mr. Jarrell in Sapporo at the beginning of this month, but I didn't have enough time to talk with him. Actually, I had one special small thing to share with him. He is from Nagoya, which has a TV tower that is a smaller version of Tokyo Tower. Sapporo has an even smaller version. Mr. Jarrell probably knows the reason why they look similar. They were all designed by the same architect, Mr. Naito. You will be surprised when you hear that Tokyo Tower was built with half as much steel as the Eiffel Tower in Paris, and Mr. Naito used a slide rule to design it, not a computer.

(Written by a reader, Sugama Takao)

architect　建築士　　the Eiffel Tower　エッフェル塔
slide rule　計算尺

北海道胆振東部地震の直前に札幌を訪れた時，じゃれマガの読者の集まりで須釜先生に初めて会いました。名古屋のテレビ塔が日本で最も古い電波塔だと聞いて驚きました。須釜先生に言われて，この3つのテレビ塔が非常に似ていることも分かりました。

He Destroyed His Own Picture!

Have you heard of Banksy? He is a graffiti artist who paints pictures on walls in Britain and North America. No one knows who he really is. He paints his pictures in the middle of the night when no one can see him. His pictures are always surprising and often funny. Sometimes he sells his pictures with his signature. Over the weekend, there was an auction for one called "Girl with Balloon." It was sold for about one million pounds (about 150 million yen). As soon as it was sold, a shredder inside the picture frame started to cut up the picture. Banksy did it by remote control.

graffiti　落書き，グラフィティ　　　signature　サイン
auction　競売，オークション　　　shredder　シュレッダー
remote control　遠隔操作

ある日突然，ビルの外壁や家の塀にびっくりするような絵を描くのがバンクシーの特徴です。金儲けのために絵を描いているとは思えませんが，時々絵を売ることもあります。正体不明のままのバンクシーですが，今回の出来事で彼の身元の話が再燃しました。

The World's Largest Fish Market Moves

Do you know where the world's largest fish market is? It was at Tsukiji in Tokyo until last Saturday, October 6. Tourists used to come to the fish market early every morning to watch the tuna auction. In the late morning, they could walk around inside the market and look at many different kinds of fish. The restaurants just outside the market served some of the freshest fish in Tokyo. Early on Sunday, the fish vendors started moving their trucks and forklifts to the new market. You can still eat good seafood at Tsukiji, but if you want to see the tuna auction, you have to go to Toyosu.

tuna auction マグロの競り
vendor 販売業者, (ここでは)仲卸業者

築地市場

豊洲市場

市場

市場

伝統は 移転する

TOYOSU MARKET ● TOKYO

築地市場は外国人観光客でにぎわっていました。特にマグロの競りは人気が高くて，僕は数年前に行こうかなと思って調べた時，朝3時に並ばないと人数制限を超えて入れないという情報を見てやめました。豊洲市場に移ってからも相変わらず人気なのでしょうか。

Even Birds Get Drunk

In a small town in the north of the United States, the birds have started acting strangely. This year, it got cold early in Minnesota. There was an early frost, and the berries on the trees started to ferment. The sugar in the berries turned to alcohol. Many birds eat these berries before they fly south for the winter. What happens to them? The alcohol makes them drunk. They can't control themselves. Some birds fall out of trees and others fly into windows or cars. The police say that you shouldn't worry if you see a drunk bird on the ground. It will wake up later and be fine.

get drunk　酔う　　Minnesota　ミネソタ州　　frost　霜
ferment　発酵する

木の実が自然に酒になったのですね。その実を食べた野鳥は、酔っぱらった人間と同じように体の動きをコントロールできなくなって木から落ちます。見てみたいと思いますが、運転している時に野鳥がフロントガラスに激突してきたら怖いですね。

A Quiz about Othello

This year, an 11-year-old boy from Kanagawa Prefecture has won the World Othello Championship. The competition was held in Prague, the Czech Republic. Fukuchi Keisuke is the youngest player to ever win the title. I didn't know that they had a World Championship. How much do you know about the game? If you know the answers, please send them to me today.

(1) How many pieces are there in the game?

(2) What color is the board?

(3) Who gave the name Othello to this game?

(4) How is the game different from Reversi?

(5) What happens if you cannot put down one of your pieces?

the World Othello Championship　世界オセロ選手権
Prague　プラハ　　piece　駒，（オセロの）石

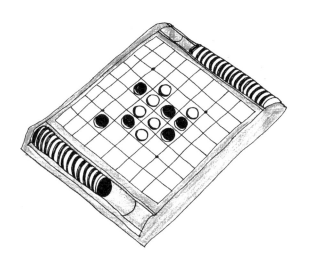

リバーシというオセロのようなボードゲームは，19世紀にイギリスで流行り，ドイツのゲーム会社が商品化しました。1970年代に長谷川五郎さんがリバーシに似たオセロを作って，今ではオセロは世界中で知られるようになりました。2018年の世界オセロ選手権には80人以上の大人と子どもが参加しました。

(1) 64 pieces.

(2) The board is green.

(3) Hasegawa Goro (or his father) did.

(4) Reversi starts with an empty board. Othello starts with four pieces on the board.

(5) You lose your turn.

Just Because They Are in Season

One of the unique things about Japan is the way people send each other fresh food in season. A friend of mine in Hokkaido sent me a box of potatoes last week. My wife's cousin, who is a farmer, sends us oranges from the farm every year. One neighbor came by my house yesterday with some persimmons that she got from her relatives. In the U.S., there are farms that send out fancy packages of fruit and nuts, but I've never heard of people sending boxes of fruit or vegetables to their friends just because they are in season.

in season 食べごろの，旬の　　persimmon　柿

アメリカ人より日本人の方が季節に敏感ですね。アメリカは広くて，どこかで野菜を作っているから，いつでも食べられる気がします。日本に来る前は「旬」ということを意識して買い物をしたことがあまりありませんでした。

Plastic Garbage

After so much rain and so many typhoons, it felt great to be outside this weekend. Yesterday was sunny, and I spent the day at Fujimae Tidal Flat with a group of children. The area was cleaner than usual because of a large clean-up event by more than 1,000 volunteers the day before. Even so, our small group of children still found plastic garbage hidden in the reeds that grow along the rivers. Plastic can be very dangerous for living things because they try to eat it. The children came back wondering why adults can't be more thoughtful about the environment and more careful with their garbage.

reed　アシ　　environment　環境

 10月27日に「藤前干潟クリーン大作戦」というイベントがあり，1000人以上のボランティアがゴミ拾いをしました。それでも次の日に子どもがプラスチックごみを見つけました。プラスチックごみを出さないような社会を作りたいと僕は思いました。

The World Series Winner Is ….

The Boston Red Sox have won the World Series! They had the best record of any team in the regular season, and they beat the Los Angeles Dodgers four games to one. Boston won the first two games at their home stadium where the temperatures went down to 7 degrees. Then the teams moved to Los Angeles where it was a much more comfortable 24 degrees. Game 3 turned into the longest game in the history of the World Series. It lasted for 7 hours and 20 minutes and went on for 18 innings! The Dodgers finally got the winning run, but that was their only win. The Red Sox went on to win Games 4 and 5.

 レッドソックスは強いですね！　でも，天気も味方
をしてくれたようです。暖かいロサンゼルスでプ
レーするドジャースは，ボストンの寒さに勝てず，
レッドソックスが最初の2試合で連勝しました。ド
ジャースはロサンゼルスへ戻っての第3戦に勝ち
ましたが，その試合はワールドシリーズ史上最も長い
試合となりました。

Trick or Treat!

Today is Halloween. It is becoming more popular in Japan, but how is it celebrated in the U.S.? Let's look at some numbers to find out. What do most people do on Halloween in the U.S.? About 70% of people celebrating Halloween said that they handed out candy to children in the neighborhood who come by and say "Trick or treat!" Almost 50% dress up in costumes, and about the same number carve pumpkins. Less than one-third actually go trick-or-treating. That is because trick-or-treating is for children, not for adults. I was surprised to see that 18% put costumes on their pets!

hand out　配る　　carve　彫る

Trick or treat!!

僕が小さい時，ハロウィンは子どものためのものでした。近所の家を回って，一生懸命お菓子を集めるのが楽しみでした。最近は，大人が主役の仮装パーティーやペットにまで衣装を着せるというニュースを聞くので，年齢に関係のないお祭りになったようです。

How Does He Do It?

Do you know the actor, Suzuki Ryohei? He is starring in the NHK historical drama on Sunday night called "Segodon." He plays Saigo Takamori. He is not only good at acting. He can gain and lose a lot of weight so that he looks like the people that he plays. He usually weighs 76 kilograms. When he played a sick man in "The Emperor's Cook," he lost 20 kilograms. Then for his next film, he gained 30 kilograms. How does he do this? He uses a small spoon and eats slowly when he wants to lose weight. When he wants to gain weight, he wakes up in the middle of the night and eats another meal. Then he goes back to sleep.

historical drama　史劇, 大河ドラマ　　play　（役などを）演じる
gain weight　体重を増やす　　lose weight　体重を減らす

鈴木亮平さんはさまざまな役でテレビや映画に出ているので，どれだけ過酷な体づくりに臨んでいるか，作品を見れば分かります。普通の人は２，３キロでもなかなか痩せられないのに，「天皇の料理番」のために鈴木さんは 20 キロも痩せました。太る時は筋肉トレーニングも行います。とても真似できません！

Buzzwords from 2018

They have just put out a list of 30 Japanese buzzwords for 2018. I like the one about the soccer player Osako, "*hampa naitte*," but will it get the grand prize in the buzzwords contest? We have to wait until December to find out. What are some English buzzwords this year? I found one word that comes from Japanese, "ninja." Of course, it doesn't mean a spy from the Edo Period. It means "expert" as in "He is a sales ninja," another way of saying "an expert salesperson." Another buzzword is "salty." It isn't used for food. It is used for people who are angry. For example, "My girlfriend is really salty today because I forgot her birthday."

buzzword　流行語

hampa naitte

ninja

salty

ビジネスの世界で「ninja」という言葉を聞いたことは
ありますが、「salty」は流行語を調べていたら出てき
ました。英語圏に住んでいないと耳にしないかも
しれません。「半端ないって」は英語で何というの
でしょうか? ある先生は「Amazing!」とか「Impres-
sive!」と訳していました。

Unique Pen Pals

I have a pen-friend. We write letters in English even though she is Japanese and we live in the same town. We studied English at the same school about 10 years ago. One day, she asked me to be her pen pal. She liked to write in English. I also wanted to use English more. We write once or twice a month. I think we have written over 100 letters so far. Nowadays, people use email or SNS to contact each other, but I'm very happy to find a letter in my mailbox. I also enjoy choosing letter paper. We may be out of date, and our English may not have improved, but we'll keep on writing letters.

(Written by a reader, Suzuki Michiyo)

out of date　時代遅れの

English

SNSやメールは手紙を書くほど手間はかかりませ
んが、郵便受けに手紙を見つけるとうれしいですね。
手紙を書く人によると、便箋や封筒に貼る切手を選
ぶのも楽しいそうです。英語をスペルチェック無し
で書く場合はスペリングの練習にもなります！

1111

Yesterday was November 11. We can write this date in numbers: 1111. What does it look like? To Japanese, it looks like Pocky sticks. To Koreans, it looks like Pepero sticks. To Chinese, it looks like four single people. Each country has a different name for the day: Pocky Day, Pepero Day and Singles Day. The names are different, but this is a day to bring people together. Many single people in China have "blind" dates. They have a date with someone they have never met before. In Japan and Korea, people share Pocky and Pepero with each other, and some men and women play the Pocky or Pepero game.

 アジアで流行っているスティック菓子ですが，アメリカでは今までに見たことはありません。アメリカでポッキーを買いたい人のために，アメリカのグリコは FIND POCKY という Web サービスを提供していて，ポッキーを販売している店を簡単に見つけることができます。

No Ordinary Junior High School Teacher

I was invited to talk to teachers in Tokyo last Saturday. They belong to a study group called Kita-Ken, which is short for Kitahara Kenkyukai. It is led by Kitahara Nobuaki, a junior high school teacher in Tokyo. He is no ordinary junior high school teacher. He has written books about teaching English and travels all over Japan to talk to other teachers. I had a chance to watch him teach. I was impressed because his third-year junior high students read one Jaremaga story silently for only one minute and were able to understand the general meaning. What a great teacher!

ordinary　普通の　　study group　研究会　　general meaning　趣旨

 北原延晃先生は，毎朝じゃれマガが届くと生徒のために
ワークシートを作ります。授業では生徒に読む
時間を1分しか与えず，1つの質問に答えさせます。
この訓練で読む速度が速くなり，読解力が身につく
ので，中学校3年生の間に英検2級に合格する生徒
も少なくありません。

Butterfly Weather

The autumn has been warm recently, so it is difficult to know what to wear. You can see some people in sweaters and jackets. Others are still wearing lighter clothes. The leaves on the trees in the city streets have started to change color, but they don't seem as beautiful this year. The warm weather has also brought back butterflies. On a sunny day, you can see them flying around looking for flowers. Why are they still here? Some butterflies like the chestnut tiger fly south for the winter, but the butterflies we are seeing now usually hibernate.

chestnut tiger　アサギマダラ　　hibernate　冬眠する

 暖かい日が続いてチョウが飛び回っています。「チョウは夏」というイメージを持っていたので，11月中旬にまだいることに驚きました。秋なのに暖かいので，渡りや冬眠をためらっているのかもしれません。

How Many Kinds of Seaweed Do You Eat?

How many kinds of seaweed do you eat? That's a good question for people in East Asia because they use seaweed in their cooking. There are some areas of Europe and Canada where seaweed is eaten, and the Maori in New Zealand eat it, too. If you ask an American this question, however, they will probably say, "We don't eat seaweed!" Japan has at least seven kinds of seaweed: *kombu*, *wakame*, *nori*, *hijiki*, *mozuku*, *umibudo*, and *arame*. My students always want to know how to say the names in English, but I tell them that they don't usually have English names. They only have scientific names that no one knows.

seaweed　海藻　　Maori　マオリ族　　scientific name　学名

kombu

wakame

hijiki

arame

mozuku

nori

umibudo

日本人はおそらく全世界で一番多く海藻類を食べる民族でしょう。この話に出てくる海藻類は英語圏の人々には親しみがなく，学名しかありません。どの種類でも海藻(seaweed)と言います。「海藻は食べ物じゃない！」と思うアメリカ人がほとんどです。

My Seventh Year of Growing Sweet Potatoes

I made ridges 30cm high and planted three types of potato on May 3 this year: *beniazuma*, *beniharuka* and *kintoki*. Last year I only planted *beniharuka*. By June 16, the *beniazuma* and *kintoki* had become larger, but the *beniharuka* were not growing well. The potatoes had a lot of leaves this year because of the heat, so I turned over the vines, something called *tsurugaeshi* in Japanese. This makes the potatoes bigger. I harvested the potatoes on October 28. Now I am planting onions and turnips where the sweet potatoes were. After I harvest them, I will make ridges again and plant more sweet potatoes.

(Written by a reader, Yanai Hirokazu)

ridge　うね　　harvest　収穫する　　turnip　カブ

kintoki

beniazuma

beniharuka

サツマイモを育てている読者が3種類の芋を植えました。1種類はだめになったかもしれませんが，他の2種類は無事に育ったようです。つる返しという方法を使うと，より良い芋が作れるそうです。畑を休ませずにどんどん作物を作ることができるので良い土なのでしょう。

She Wanted a Japanese Radish

A festival was held at an agriculture center in Nagoya on Nov. 3. When we got there at 10 a.m., many people were shopping and eating. There were a lot of stalls with vegetables, fruit and other farm products. We bought persimmons, honey, Japanese leaf tea and pumpkins. My wife really wanted to buy a Japanese radish, but she decided to buy it later because it was heavy. We walked around and saw many farm animals. A calf was born on Sep. 20, and they wanted everyone to give her a name. We went back to the stalls, but to my wife's great disappointment, the Japanese radishes were sold out.

(Written by a reader, Goto Yasuhiro)

agriculture center　農業センター　　farm product　農産物
calf　子牛

朝市に行って，重たい大根を持って歩き回りたくないので買うのを後回しにしたら，買いそびれてしまいました。気持ちは分かりますが，もったいないことをしましたね！　結局近くのスーパーへ行って大根を買ったのでしょうか。

Two of BBC's 100 Women

Every year BBC makes a list of 100 special women. Some of them are leaders, some are people with great ideas, some have started groups to help others, and some are everyday heroes. This year, there are two Japanese women on the list. Takamizawa Setsuko is 90 years old, but she has started learning English so that she can help tourists who will come to the Tokyo Olympics. That's amazing at her age! Okoda Yuki is also on the list. She is only 23 years old, but she has already made an important discovery that may help other physicists understand how our solar system began.

physicist　物理学者　　solar system　太陽系

BBCの「100人の女性」は全世界から選ばれています。この2人の日本人以外にも，クリントン元大統領の娘チェルシーさんや，インドネシア初の女性ムスリム漫談師，ラオスのラグビーコーチなど，あらゆる場で活躍している女性が含まれています。

18 Weird Things That Only Exist in Japan

There is a video on YouTube called "18 Weird Things That Only Exist in Japan." These things seem very strange to Americans. I'll tell you about three of them. If you are interested, you can go to YouTube and see the rest. (1) You can turn around the seats on trains when you want to sit in a group of four. I've never seen seats like that on trains in any other country. (2) Water comes out of the top of the toilet. You can wash your hands with it, and it's a good way to save water. (3) One fast-food chain made a special hamburger holder for women who want to cover their faces when they eat hamburgers.

weird　変な　　hamburger holder　バーガー袋

自分の国にないものを不思議に思うことは変ではありません。(1) と (2) は実用的で他の国にもあったらいいなと思いますが，長年日本に住んでいる僕でさえ，(3) は不思議で仕方がありません。

Dec. 10, 2018

Meet the New Champion

Even though this was Kihira Rika's first season skating as a senior, she won two events and was able to go on to the ISU Grand Prix of Figure Skating Final. She was competing against last year's champion, Alina Zagitova. In the short program, Kihira got the highest score of any woman skater this year. In the free program, she fell once, but she kept the lead and got the gold medal. She is the first Japanese skater since Asada Mao to win in a Grand Prix Final in her debut season. Now Kihira is looking ahead not only to next year but also to the 2022 Beijing Winter Olympics. She dreams of winning the gold medal there.

keep the lead　首位を保つ

紀平梨花選手は安定していて，あまりミスをしない選手です。見ていて安心します。10代で世界に注目されているプレッシャーに負けない紀平選手は素晴らしいですね。

You'd Better Be Good!

Christmas is only 11 days away. Are you going to get a present this year? That depends on whether you are good or bad. If you are good, Santa Claus will bring you presents. What if you are bad? In some central European countries, you won't meet Santa Claus. Instead, you will meet a big demon called Krampus. He is very hairy and has large horns. Krampus comes to see children who don't behave themselves. He gives them a piece of coal. Sometimes he even puts them in a bag and carries them away. Children, you had better be good!

demon 鬼, 悪魔　　horn 角　　behave oneself 行儀良くする

 昔から，ドイツなどの中央ヨーロッパの国々では悪い子をおどすことをしてきました。親指をしゃぶらないよう，夜中にお化けが出てきて大きなはさみで子どもの親指を切るという絵本をオーストリア人の祖母に読まされて，とても怖かった記憶があります。

Table Tennis Champions

It was a good weekend for Japan in table tennis. Harimoto Tomokazu became the youngest player to win the World Tour Grand Finals singles competition. He was ranked number 5 in the world, and in the finals he went up against Lin Gaoyuan of China, who was ranked number 4. Lin was the favorite, but Harimoto played better and won 4 out of 5 games. He had a big smile on his face when he came in first. Hayata Hina and Ito Mima were also winners. The two women were ranked number 1. They were the favorites, and they beat the Chinese team of Chen and Sun of China who were ranked third.

the World Tour Grand Finals　ワールドツアーグランドファイナル
be ranked ～　　～位にランク付けされる

卓球の張本智和選手が最年少で優勝しました。たびたび野性的な叫び声をあげるのがとても印象的ですが，彼にとって必要な行動なのでしょう。早田ひな選手と伊藤美誠選手のペアも優勝し，2020 年のオリンピックがますます楽しみです。

Keep Warm with Electric Clothing

How do people keep warm in winter? Many people wear coats, but coats can be inconvenient when you travel by car. You have to take them off when you get in and put them on again when you get out. That's why many businessmen wear vests under their suit jackets. These days, there are thin vests that are very warm because they are made of down (duck feathers). There is also electric clothing for people who are active outdoors. I met someone who was wearing an electric top (like a thin sweater). It was powered with a battery. He really liked it because it kept him very warm.

inconvenient 不便な，邪魔な   be powered with ～　～で動く

電気毛布と同じ仕組みで電気が流れると暖かくなる
ベストですね。きっと安全に着られるものだと思い
ますが、なんだか不安です。もしも水に濡れたら感
電死につながるのではないでしょうか？　僕なら羽
毛のベストで十分です。

Two Christmas Cards

READER A: I got a Christmas card from my daughter-in-law. The Christmas card plays "We Wish You a Merry Christmas" as the lights blink on and off. Once, my husband turned on the switch when I got upset, and I calmed down. My daughter-in-law will never know that the card is so helpful!

READER B: Some Christmas cards are fantastic, some are beautiful, and some are comical. I am old and live alone. This year I received a card that played a Christmas carol. One of my friends sent it to me with a message saying that she wants me to be livelier at Christmas. With her card, I can't stop smiling.

(Written by two readers, Habu Emiko, and Ito Hiromi)

daughter-in-law　義理の娘　　blink on and off　点滅する
Christmas carol　クリスマスを祝う歌

音楽が流れるクリスマスカードをもらったことはありますが，これほど効果のあるものだとは思いませんでした。今年の冬にクリスマスカードを選ぶ時，1つの選択肢にしようと思います。

Real or Artificial?

In Japan, most Christmas trees are made of plastic. In the U.S., there are many artificial trees, but there are also many real trees. You can buy them at Christmas tree lots. In 2015, a real tree cost about 50 dollars, and an artificial tree cost a little more. Which is better, a real one or an artificial one? That depends. You can reuse artificial trees, but you have to throw away real ones. Real ones smell good, but plastic trees don't have any smell. Real trees don't use plastic, so they are probably better for the environment. If I lived in the U.S., I would buy a real tree.

artificial 人工の   reuse 再利用する

 小さい時から本物の木のクリスマスツリーばかり
使ってきましたが，日本では手ごろな値段で手に入
らないので，仕方なく人工のものを使うようになり
ました。確かに昔と比べて人工のものも良くできて
いますが，本物には及びません。

Carpool Karaoke

Karaoke is from Japan, but it is popular all over the world. There is a special karaoke skit on a late-night TV talk show. It is called "Carpool Karaoke." A British comedian named James Corden drives around Los Angeles with a famous singer. When he turns on the radio, it plays that singer's songs. Corden and the singer sing along, so it is not really karaoke, but that doesn't matter. The videos are a lot of fun. You can see many different famous American and British pop singers with him. I found videos of two of my favorite singers, Stevie Wonder and Bruno Mars.

carpool　自動車の相乗り　　skit　寸劇, スキット

車でロサンゼルスの道を走りながら有名な歌手と雑談し，その歌手の歌を突然車内で流して一緒に歌うという愉快な番組です。大学生に見せたところ，1人は「混んでいる道で危ないのでは？」と疑問を口にしました。何か工夫しているのではないかと思いますが…。

●著者略歴
Douglas S. Jarrell （ダグラス・ジャレル）
1953 年　アメリカ　ノースカロライナ州生まれ
大学の非常勤講師，藤前干潟の活動家

主な研究内容
• CALL （Computer-Assisted Language Learning,
　コンピュータを利用した言語学習）
• 異文化コミュニケーション
など

表紙イラスト：たしろさなえ
本文イラスト：尾﨑香菜子

じゃれマガ – 100 Stories of 2018
2019 年 7 月 1 日　初版第 1 刷発行

著者　　　ダグラス・ジャレル
発行元　　株式会社浜島書店
　　　　　〒 466-8691　名古屋市昭和区阿由知通 2-1-1
　　　　　電話 052（733）8040 （代）

ISBN 978-4-8343-5045-6 C0082 ¥463E